Usborne
Build your own
SPACE
WARRIORS
Sticker Book

Designed by Marc Maynard
Written by Simon Tudhope
Illustrated by Gong Studios

Contents

Mami Denja

Convicts on the prison planet Alcatrax 8 are competing in the Death Race 5000. The prize is freedom, and the notorious Mami Denja has no intention of coming second...

STATISTICS

- Skill: 7
- Bravery: 10
- Intelligence: 8
- Attack power: 6
- Home planet: Igbos

3

The Overseer

This mysterious being can travel to any point in time or space. Able to start wars in the blink of an eye, or end them before they've even begun, he maintains the balance between order and chaos across the universe.

Baldog

Baldog is the undefeated champion of the GGG (Galactic Gladiator Games). Competitors from the four corners of the galaxy have tried and failed to best him in a brutal fight to the finish.

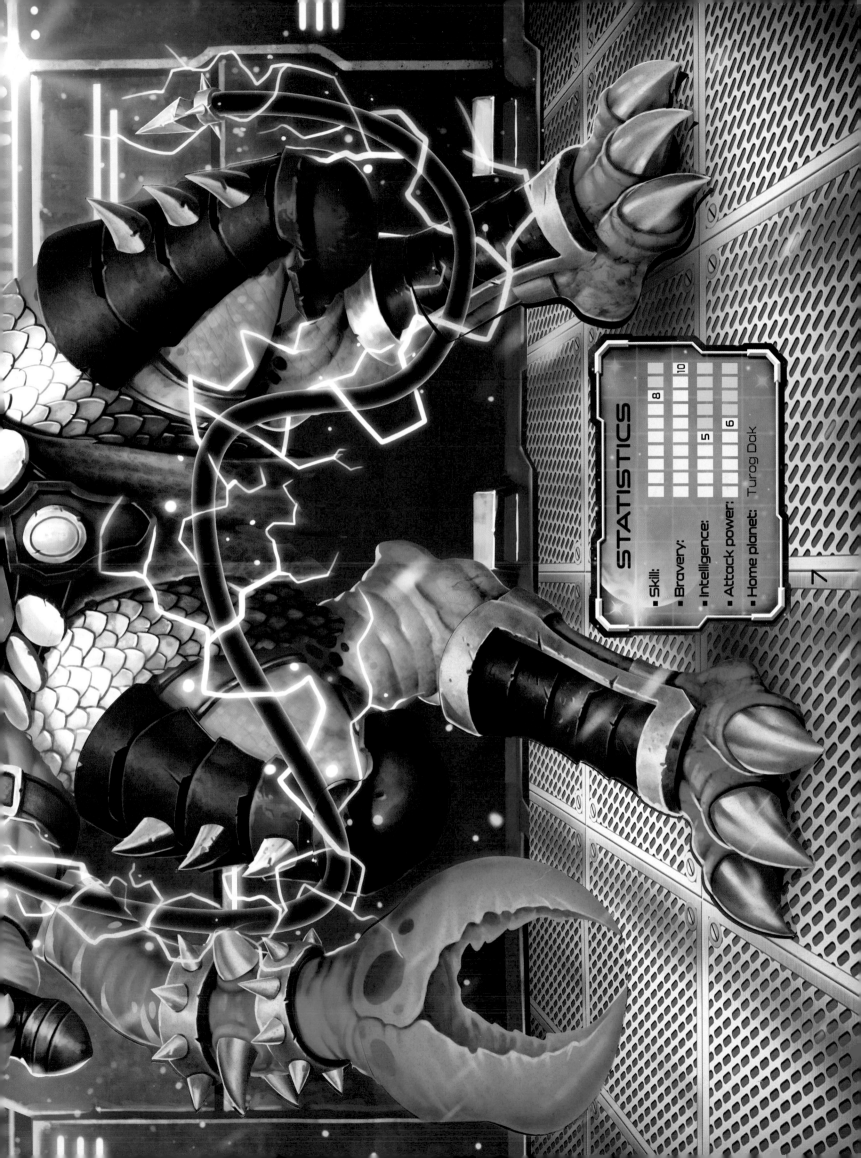

STATISTICS

- Skill:
- Bravery:
- Intelligence: 5
- Attack power: 6
- Home planet: Turog Dak

8
10

Munika-2

Munika-2 has hacked the primary supercomputer of the Karzen fleet. Rewriting billions of commands a second, she disables their weapons systems and downs their shields. Outside, space lights up with exploding ships.

STATISTICS

- Skill:
- Bravery:
- Intelligence:
- Attack power:
- Home planet: Volton

Frolix

Frolix was a small alien with three eyes...
until his mind was transferred into this
mechanized hulk. Now he's the ultimate war
machine. "THE INVASION ENDS HERE!"
his robotic voice crackles. "IT ENDS NOW!"

STATISTICS

- Skill: 5
- Bravery: 7
- Intelligence: 8
- Attack power: 8
- Home planet: Marlosa

Nemesar

The most feared bounty hunter in the galaxy closes on her target. Her drones have tracked him down to Giga City 3. Soon the documents he stole will be secret once more, and he'll face a simple question: "Dead or alive, Drakan Tor? The choice is yours."

STATISTICS

- Skill:
- Bravery: 6
- Intelligence: 8
- Attack power: 6
- Home planet: Nexus

8

Yantar

The ancient prophecies foretold this moment, when the stones would burn with strange symbols and a portal would open from another dimension. Yantar, destroyer of worlds, has come at last.

STATISTICS

- Skill: 8
- Bravery: 8
- Intelligence: 8
- Attack power: 10
- Home planet: unknown

15

Greezo

Meet the first pilot to shoot down an enemy ship in hyperspace, the first to slingshot around a black hole, the second to navigate the minefields surrounding Malgon-5 (but the first to survive). With her lightning reflexes and 360-degree vision, Greezo is the galaxy's undisputed top gun.

STATISTICS

- Skill: 10
- Bravery: 9
- Intelligence: 8
- Attack power: 7
- Home planet: Hive-362C

Captain Vance

The ancient buildings of New London were reduced to rubble many centuries ago, but the war still rages on. Captain Vance is Earth's most decorated hero. Leading a daring raid on an enemy camp, he drives the aliens back beyond the city walls.

STATISTICS

▪ Skill:							7		
▪ Bravery:									10
▪ Intelligence:								8	
▪ Attack power:						6			
▪ Home planet:	Earth								

Garstang Lode

It'll take more than a few GP (Galactic Police) gunships to bring this fugitive to justice. Lode is the only prisoner to have broken out of the maximum security Void Cage, and he's evaded capture ever since.

STATISTICS

- Skill: 8
- Bravery: 9
- Intelligence: 9
- Attack power: 6
- Home planet: Yojimbo

The Acrida

These alien cyborgs fly through space like a plague of locusts. They move from planet to planet, landing in their millions and turning whole worlds to dust.

STATISTICS

- Skill: 6
- Bravery: 6
- Intelligence: 7
- Attack power: 10
- Home planet: Arbeh

Glossary

- **360-degree vision:** the power to see in all directions at once

- **black hole:** a point in space that pulls everything towards it, a bit like a whirlpool. Stars, planets, even light itself are all sucked in and destroyed.

- **convict:** a convicted criminal

- **cyborg:** part-alien (or human) and part-machine

- **dimension:** "another dimension" means a different universe from our own

- **drone:** a machine that's controlled from a distance

- **fugitive:** a criminal on the loose

- **hack:** break into a secure computer system

- **hyperspace:** a place where you can travel faster than the speed of light

- **locust:** an insect that often flies in huge swarms which can devour whole fields of crops

- **notorious:** famous for something bad

- **prophecy:** a prediction about the future

Edited by Sam Taplin
Additional design and digital manipulation by Keith Furnival

First published in 2020 by Usborne Publishing Ltd, Usborne House, 83-85 Saffron Hill, London EC1N 8RT, England. www.usborne.com